Original title:

Raindrops Running Through Rainbows

Copyright © 2024 Creative Arts Management OÜ
All rights reserved.

Author: Aidan Marlowe
ISBN HARDBACK: 978-9916-90-710-8
ISBN PAPERBACK: 978-9916-90-711-5

Chromatic Tears from the Heavens

In twilight skies where colors blend,
A spectrum falls, our hearts transcend.
Each drop a tale, a dream anew,
Chromatic tears, the world in hue.

With every splash, the ground awakes,
Awash in shades, the silence breaks.
A canvas formed from nature's heart,
In radiant bursts, we find our part.

Symphony of Hues and Deluge

A melody of colors rain,
In ceaseless dance, they charm the plain.
Each note a hue that lights the night,
A symphony of pure delight.

With whispered winds, the colors play,
As droplets shimmer, fall, and sway.
In harmony, the world does sing,
A vibrant song, a wondrous spring.

Celestial Drizzles upon a Radiant Loom

The heavens weave their gentle threads,
In drizzles soft, where beauty spreads.
Each strand a spark of light and grace,
Upon the loom, a warm embrace.

With every drop, the fabric glows,
In colors bright, the essence flows.
Celestial art upon the ground,
A masterpiece where joy is found.

Nature's Paintbrush on a Silver Canvas

With every stroke, the Earth renews,
A paintbrush dipped in vibrant hues.
Upon the silver, colors dance,
Nature's art, a fleeting chance.

In whispers soft, the palette bursts,
As golden rays and azure thrusts.
Each moment fleeting, yet sublime,
A timeless tale, a story's rhyme.

The Mirth of Saturated Air

In the hush of evening's glow,
Raindrops dance, a gentle show.
Whispers float on scented breeze,
Nature's laughter, hearts appease.

Colors blur in twilight's hue,
Life revived, the world feels new.
In this warmth, we breathe, we share,
Boundless joy in saturated air.

Glimmering Footprints in the Storm

Amidst the shadows, thunder claps,
We trace our steps in puddles' laps.
Each footprint glimmers, bold and bright,
A map of moments in the night.

Winds of change swirl all around,
In chaos, beauty can be found.
Through stormy paths, we carry on,
With glimmering footprints 'til the dawn.

Crafting Magic in the Moisture

With every droplet, dreams entwine,
In droplets' dance, the stars align.
A canvas draped in misty lace,
Casting spells in every space.

Hands wet with wonder, hearts ablaze,
In stylish storms, we weave our ways.
A world transformed, the magic flows,
In every breath, the moisture glows.

Canvas of Liquid Skies

Above the world, the colors play,
Soft whispers dance in hues of gray.
Golden suns and silver streams,
Awake the heart, inspire dreams.

Clouds drift on, so light and free,
Painted wild, like thoughts at sea.
Every stroke tells nature's tale,
A canvas large, where breezes sail.

Shimmering Threads of Nature

In the woods, a tapestry,
Woven bright with life's decree.
Leaves that flutter, petals glow,
Nature's heart begins to show.

Streams that shimmer, softly sing,
Threads of peace that nature brings.
In each fold, a story waits,
Guiding souls through nature's gates.

Twilight's Drizzle of Joy

As twilight falls, the world will pause,
A gentle drizzle without cause.
Joy spills forth like drops of rain,
Cleansing hearts from worry's stain.

Stars emerge with twinkling grace,
Filling night's vast, open space.
In the quiet, laughter stirs,
As joy in drizzles softly purrs.

Colors Soaked in Melody

In every shade, a melody,
Colors dance in harmony.
Glistening notes upon the air,
Painting feelings everywhere.

Brushes sweep with vibrant sound,
Where the heart and art are bound.
Songs of joy and gentle sighs,
Echo in the painted skies.

Beads of Spectral Delight

Tiny spheres of light,
Dancing on the breeze,
Whispers of the night,
Carried by the trees.

Colors swirl and blend,
Glimmer in the dark,
Nature's hand extends,
Crafting a small spark.

In this tranquil space,
Magic starts to play,
With a gentle grace,
They twirl and sway.

Moments held so brief,
Like a sweet refrain,
Beads of pure belief,
In joy and in pain.

The Play of Sun and Saturation

Golden rays descend,
Kissing earth so warm,
Nature's light to send,
Creating every form.

In fields of lush green,
Colors burst alive,
A vibrant scene seen,
Where all dreams arrive.

With shadows that dance,
And patterns that gleam,
Every fleeting chance,
Is a painter's dream.

At sunset's last sigh,
The sky softly glows,
While day waves goodbye,
And night gently flows.

Charm of the Wandering Droplets

Gentle pearls of rain,
Trickle down the pane,
Each one holds a tale,
Of whispers in the frail.

On petals they land,
Kissing with a sigh,
Caressing the land,
Beneath the cloudy sky.

They wander so free,
In a dance divine,
A fluidity,
That feels like a sign.

With laughter they play,
In the morning light,
Chasing clouds away,
A joyous delight.

The Art of Wet Reflections

Mirrors of the sky,
In puddles they greet,
As clouds drift on by,
Where earth and dreams meet.

Images transform,
Warped in liquid glass,
In every soft storm,
Moments seem to pass.

With ripples that trace,
A story profound,
In this tranquil space,
Harmony is found.

Embracing the scene,
A canvas of grace,
In the spaces between,
Time leaves not a trace.

Clarity in the Chaos

In shadows deep, where whispers blend,
Truth emerges, soft and clear.
Amidst the noise, where dreams ascend,
A light will guide, dispelling fear.

Through tangled paths, the heart can see,
Moments still, where silence speaks.
In every storm, there's harmony,
A gentle peace that love seeks.

Voices lost, yet hearts collide,
In swirling winds, we find our place.
Together strong, we turn the tide,
Embracing now, with endless grace.

In chaos' grip, we learn to dance,
Finding clarity within the strife.
With every heartbeat, take a chance,
To see the beauty in this life.

The Essence of Hues and Storms

Clouds gather with colors bright,
Painting skies in vivid dreams.
Lightning dances, a fleeting light,
Nature speaks in vibrant themes.

Crimson whispers, cobalt cries,
Each hue tells a story bold.
From the storms, the spirit flies,
In rainbows formed, our hearts unfold.

Amidst the tempest, we ignite,
Fires of passion, fierce and free.
In every gust, a spark of light,
A canvas born of stormy sea.

With each new dawn, we seek and find,
The magic found in every storm.
In essence, hearts and colors bind,
Creating beauty, love transforms.

Hearts Raining Down Light

In gentle drops, our love will flow,
Carving paths through life's vast sea.
As hearts collide, their warmth will glow,
Together, shining endlessly.

Like sunlit beams through dreary skies,
Each moment shared, a tender spark.
In every laugh, in every sigh,
We scatter light; we leave our mark.

When shadows fall and darkness fades,
Our spirits lift, a radiant flight.
In every storm, the joy cascades,
Hearts raining down a world of light.

In union soft, we stand as one,
Illuminated by our fire.
With every dawn, new dreams are spun,
Hearts intertwined, our great desire.

Ruins in the Wake of Spectrum

In echoes lost, the past remains,
Fragments scattered, tales untold.
Beneath the colors, beauty wanes,
Within the ruins, stories unfold.

A tapestry of joy and pain,
Dusty paths where hopes have grown.
In every hue, a bittersweet strain,
Remnants of love that were once sown.

Through shattered dreams, we seek the light,
In every crack, a spark survives.
From wreckage born, we rise from fright,
Embracing change, our spirit thrives.

In the spectrum's end, there's grace,
A palette rich with life reborn.
From ruins, we reclaim our space,
And weave anew from tales of torn.

Whispers of Color in the Storm

Gray clouds roll in, a canvas wide,
Electric flashes, nature's guide.
Whispers of color, hues so bright,
Dance in the shadows, a fleeting light.

Raindrops falling, a soothing sound,
Each splash of color spills around.
In the tempest, beauty will find,
A masterpiece shaped by the wind's mind.

The thunder rumbles, a distant song,
In the chaos, we feel we belong.
A heart ignites with every strike,
Whispers of color, a vibrant dyke.

When the storm fades, rainbows appear,
Framed in whispers, bold yet clear.
Nature's palette, a wondrous show,
In the aftermath, the colors glow.

Prism's Embrace in Waterfall's Breath

Water tumbles with a gentle sigh,
Cascading light where shadows lie.
Prism's embrace in the misty air,
Colors merge, a world laid bare.

Silver droplets, a curtain of grace,
Reflecting hues in a timeless space.
Echoing softly, a song of peace,
In nature's dance, all worries cease.

The sun breaks through, igniting streams,
In waterfalls, we find our dreams.
Every splash a lucky charm,
Nature whispers, enchanting and warm.

Glimmers of magic, a fleeting glance,
A radiant ballet, the water's dance.
In the heart of nature, we breathe free,
Bathed in prisms, wild and carefree.

Dancing Puddles beneath a Kaleidoscope Sky

Puddles shimmer, a playful sight,
Mirroring clouds, dancing light.
Beneath a sky, so vast and bold,
A symphony of colors unfold.

Children laugh, splashing about,
In joyful dance, they scream and shout.
Kaleidoscope dreams in every blink,
In every puddle, lost in drink.

Raindrops glisten, an art divine,
Reflecting stories in every line.
Each ripple tells a tale so grand,
Of laughter shared and moments planned.

As twilight sets, the colors shift,
Nature's painting, a cherished gift.
Dancing puddles, a heart's delight,
Beneath the stars, in soft twilight.

Liquid Arches in the Tempest's Glow

Clouds gather, swirling in dismay,
A tempest brews in sky's dark play.
Liquid arches, bending light,
In the chaos, beauty takes flight.

Raindrops race down every lane,
Each one a drop of joy, a chain.
With every flash, the night ignites,
In stormy whispers, hidden sights.

Colors bleed, as shadows blend,
In liquid arches, the heavens bend.
Nature's fury sings a song,
In tumult's grip, we all belong.

When quiet comes, and darkness fades,
A world awash with light cascades.
The tempest's glow, a tender show,
In liquid arches, love will grow.

Chasing Liquid Prisms

In a world where colors blend,
A splash of light begins to bend.
Reflections dance upon the stream,
Chasing shadows in a dream.

Rippling echoes in soft array,
Fleeting moments drift away.
Each drop holds stories yet untold,
A canvas spun from hues of gold.

Fingers trace the glassy flow,
Discovering depths where secrets grow.
Luminous whispers kiss the air,
Every breath a vibrant flare.

With wandering eyes, we chase the light,
Through liquid prisms, bold and bright.
In the spectrum's tender guise,
We find our truth beneath the skies.

A Dance of Celestial Hues

Stars awaken in the night,
Painting darkness with their light.
Galaxies swirl in a graceful twirl,
Cosmic secrets unfurl and unfurl.

Nebulas bloom in colors rare,
Whispers carried through the air.
A ballet spun in cosmic grace,
Every twinkle finds its place.

Planets twine in silent waltz,
Orbiting dreams, no faults.
In this dance of endless skies,
We witness beauty in their rise.

Celestial hues ignite the soul,
Filling hearts, making them whole.
Lost in wonder, we stand amazed,
At the dance the universe plays.

Syllables of Sky and Water

Rippling waves call out my name,
Syllables echo without shame.
The sky reflects in liquid blue,
As nature sings its timeless tune.

Clouds drift softly, whisper low,
Carrying tales that ebb and flow.
In the quiet, my heart takes flight,
Dancing between day and night.

Raindrops fall, a gentle kiss,
Each one a note of tranquil bliss.
Sky and water in harmony,
Compose a song, sweet and free.

With every breeze, a stanza forms,
Embracing the calm through all storms.
In the melody of earth and air,
I find my peace, my spirit bare.

Melodies in a Prism

Sunlight streams through crystal glass,
Creating colors as it passes.
A symphony of hues doth play,
In laughter of the light's ballet.

Every spectrum sings a song,
Harmonies where hearts belong.
Dancing rays on walls and floors,
Unlocking dreams behind closed doors.

Each angle turns a note anew,
In prismatic bliss, the world imbues.
Reflections shimmer with soft delight,
Leading us through the endless night.

In this prism, joy unfolds,
Melodies of stories told.
A vibrant world, alive and bright,
Where every moment feels just right.

Reflections in the Puddle

In still water lies the sky,
Shimmering clouds float by.
Fragments of dreams take flight,
In puddles, worlds ignite.

Footsteps dance with delight,
Mirroring day to night.
Each drop a tale it tells,
In gentle laughter, it dwells.

Shadows shift, redefine,
True colors intertwine.
A fleeting glimpse of grace,
In nature's soft embrace.

Reflections paint the ground,
Where silence can be found.
In every drop a muse,
The art the rain can choose.

The Melody of Mist and Hue

Whispers drift in the dawn,
Colors wake on the lawn.
Gentle mists weave and sway,
Nature's song at play.

Brushes dipped in the sky,
Painted whispers glide by.
In every shade a story,
A canvas of pure glory.

Soft notes of lavender blend,
With emeralds that extend.
Each hue a fleeting sigh,
A melody to comply.

As daylight greets the trees,
The symphony flows with ease.
In harmony, they blend,
Nature's song without end.

Fluid Whispers of Color

Emerald leaves softly sway,
Beneath the sun's warm ray.
Crimson blooms catch the eye,
In gardens where dreams lie.

Flowing rivers hum their tune,
Mirrored under the moon.
A tapestry of bright light,
Whispers threading the night.

A dance of shades takes flight,
With shadows weaving tight.
In the stillness they glide,
Where secrets can abide.

Ebb and flow, colors blend,
In nature, hearts transcend.
Each whisper softly sings,
The beauty that joy brings.

Nature's Caress in the Downpour

Raindrops kiss the thirsty earth,
Awakening life with mirth.
In each patter, peace is found,
Earth's heartbeat, gentle sound.

Clouds embrace with tender care,
Drifting whispers fill the air.
Nourishing roots underground,
Harmony all around.

Leaves drink deep, a joyful hush,
In the rush, hearts start to flush.
A symphony of life unfolds,
In droplets, stories told.

Nature's grace through every storm,
Wrapped in warmth, we transform.
In the downpour, we rejoice,
Hearing earth's authentic voice.

The Waters' Kaleidoscope

Rippling hues in gentle sway,
Reflections dance, the light's bouquet.
Colors mingle, soft and bright,
Nature's palette in sheer delight.

Waves create a rhythmic song,
In the flow, we all belong.
Shadows play upon the shore,
Whispers call us to explore.

Mirrors of the sky above,
Tales of earth, and dreams of love.
Each droplet holds a world unseen,
In the waters, life's serene.

Glistening gems that ebb and flow,
Holding secrets we long to know.
In the depths, where wonders lie,
The waters' kiss, a soft goodbye.

Spirit of Drops and Light

Tiny orbs of liquid grace,
Dance on petals, find their place.
Glistening in the morning sun,
Life awakens, day's begun.

With a shimmer, they arise,
Gifts of nature, sweet surprise.
Sprinkled joys in verdant fields,
Each one whispers what it yields.

Light refracts in colors bright,
Creating worlds with pure delight.
Every drop, a story told,
In the spirit, moments hold.

Beneath the touch of sighing breeze,
Harmony in soft rustles frees.
Drops like jewels on emerald leaves,
In such beauty, the heart believes.

Beyond the Veil of Vapor

Misty shadows cloak the dawn,
Veils of wonder, gently drawn.
Secrets drift on morning air,
Whispers roam without a care.

In the haze, the world transforms,
Nature dances, soft and warm.
Fleeting forms, a dreamlike flight,
In the vapor, pure delight.

Stories linger, lost and found,
In the silence, echoes sound.
Ghostly figures glimmer faint,
Brush of shadows, sweet constraint.

Beyond the mist, the sun breaks free,
Painting skies in reverie.
Every droplet, each embrace,
Holds reflection, time and space.

Cascading Dreams of Spectrum

Ribbons of light cascade and flow,
Whispers of colors, soft and low.
Dreams that travel on a breeze,
Flowing gently through the trees.

Each hue dances, bold and bright,
In the twilight, pure delight.
Rainbows weave through skies of gray,
Legendary paths we lay.

Moments drip in vibrant streams,
Carving out our wildest dreams.
Cascades of hope, love's embrace,
Painting time in endless grace.

Falling stars in evening's hue,
Nature's magic, ever true.
In this dream, we float and soar,
Cascading hearts forevermore.

Echoes in the Downpour

Raindrops tap on window panes,
Whispering secrets of the night.
Footsteps splash in pools of dreams,
Lost in echoes, sheer delight.

Lightning dances, a fleeting glance,
Thunder rumbles, wild and deep.
Nature's symphony, a fleeting chance,
As shadows in the puddles leap.

Winds weave stories through the air,
Carrying scents of earth anew.
Each drop a memory to share,
In the downpour's soft adieu.

The Colors' Embrace in the Mist

Morning dew on blades of grass,
Colors swirl in gentle light.
Mist enfolds the world, a mask,
Painting dreams in softest white.

Amber hues kissed by the dawn,
Emerald whispers breathe with ease.
As nature wakes, the veil is drawn,
A canvas bright beneath the trees.

Wildflowers sway, a waltz so sweet,
In the embrace of fog's warm sigh.
Colors mingle where shadows meet,
In this moment, time slips by.

Tapestry of the Afterstorm

Clouds drift slowly, fading gray,
Sunlight pierces through the gloom.
Puddles glisten in a play,
As nature blooms beyond the doom.

Rainbow arches, vibrant bridge,
Binding worlds of dark and light.
Each color sings, a gentle pledge,
Healing hearts with pure delight.

Birds return with songs of cheer,
Nestled branches sway and sway.
In the calm, we hold what's dear,
A tapestry woven of today.

Liquid Light: A Love Letter

In your eyes, the stars collide,
Liquid light that warms my soul.
Every glance a gentle tide,
Pulling me towards your whole.

Whispers soft as twilight's breath,
Promises dance in the air.
With each heartbeat, I defy death,
In your love, I find my share.

Time stands still when we embrace,
Moments captured in pure gold.
In this life, our secret place,
A love letter never old.

Teardrops of Joy in a Brilliant Storm

In the heart of a tempest, soft whispers soar,
Golden raindrops shimmer, a bright encore.
Each teardrop a promise, vivid and bright,
Dancing with shadows, embracing the night.

Joy finds its rhythm in the pouring rain,
Life's weight feels lighter, releasing the pain.
Every lightning flash paints a canvas bold,
In the storm's embrace, our stories unfold.

Through the chaos, a melody sweet,
Footsteps of laughter in the storm's heartbeat.
Nature rejoices, a chorus of glee,
Mixed with the teardrops that set our hearts free.

As thunder rumbles, we raise our gaze,
Finding our fortune in the storm's wild ways.
Teardrops of joy, a spectacular view,
In the brilliant tempest, our souls feel anew.

Ethereal Melodies in a Shower of Light

When dawn spills color, soft notes appear,
The world awakens, and dreams draw near.
Ethereal whispers float on the breeze,
Singing of beauty beneath the tall trees.

In gardens of wonder, the symphony blooms,
Lights dance like fireflies, brightening rooms.
Melodies rise with the sun in the sky,
Harmonious echoes, a sweet lullaby.

With every splendor, a story unfolds,
In the shower of light, a magic it holds.
Notes shimmer and twirl, like leaves on the ground,
In ethereal realms, true peace can be found.

Let hearts open wide, and spirits ignite,
As love's gentle touch brings forth pure delight.
In showers of light, the world feels so right,
Ethereal melodies make everything bright.

Celestial Streams among Shadowed Glades

In hidden glades where the sunlight weaves,
Celestial streams flow beneath ancient leaves.
Whispers of starlight, soft shadows embrace,
Nature's own heartbeat in a sacred space.

Among the wild ferns, a soft breeze sings,
Bringing tales of hope on delicate wings.
Each droplet of light, an echo divine,
In shimmering waters, our spirits align.

Reflections of wonder dance on the waves,
Echoing dreams where the river behaves.
Through shadowed glades, paths brightly lead,
In celestial streams, our souls are freed.

With every soft ripple, the silence speaks,
Of love and the memories that nature seeks.
In these lush corners, where time holds its breath,
Celestial streams weave the whispers of death.

Vibrancy's Dance on the Edge of Hope

Upon the horizon, colors collide,
Vibrancy's dance, where dreams can abide.
With each swirling hue, the heart takes flight,
Breathing in the beauty of day and night.

In gardens of longing, petals unfold,
Stories of passion and futures to hold.
A tapestry woven of moments so bright,
On the edge of hope, we find our light.

As shadows may linger, the sun breaks through,
Painting the skies in vibrant hues.
With every new dawn, possibilities gleam,
In the dance of life, we awaken our dream.

With rhythm and grace, we rise from the fall,
Embracing the magic that beckons us all.
On the edge of hope, where our spirits prance,
In vibrancy's dance, we seize every chance.

The Ebb and Flow of Radiance

In the dawn's gentle light,
Shadows dance with grace,
Whispers of a new day,
Bathed in soft embrace.

Waves of warmth arise,
Kissing the morning dew,
Each ray a tender touch,
As colors break through.

Evening drapes its cloak,
Stars begin to gleam,
In the silence of night,
We unravel a dream.

The cycle of brilliance,
Through dusk and through dawn,
The ebb and the flow,
In radiance, we are drawn.

Vivid Tides of Emotion

Ride the waves of feeling,
A swell of the heart,
Tides that rise and fall,
In shades of love's art.

Crimson brushes the sky,
In a tempest so bold,
Soft touches of joy,
And stories untold.

The ocean's deep longing,
A rhythm that sways,
With currents of laughter,
In passionate plays.

Through storms we discover,
What's buried below,
Vivid tides of emotion,
In waves that still flow.

Fantasia Born from the Clouds

Clouds weave dreams in the sky,
With colors that blend,
A tapestry of wonder,
Where visions ascend.

From silver linings bright,
To shadows that part,
Fantasia takes flight,
With wings of the heart.

Soft whispers of laughter,
On breezes so light,
Each moment a painting,
In day and in night.

A realm where we wander,
In fantasies grand,
Born from the clouds,
In a magical land.

Brilliant Cascades of Joy

Joy pours like a river,
In cascades so bright,
With laughter as bubbles,
In the warm morning light.

Gentle streams of delight,
Flow through every heart,
Each drop a reminder,
Of love's perfect art.

Dancing leaves on the air,
In a symphony's play,
Brilliant cascades of joy,
Guide us along the way.

With each moment we cherish,
New wonders arise,
In the beauty of living,
Where happiness lies.

Symphony of the Deluge

Raindrops fall like gentle sighs,
Nature sings beneath grey skies.
Thunder rumbles, a distant drum,
While rivers swell, their currents hum.

Lightning dances, a fleeting spark,
Illuminating shadows dark.
Amid the storm, the world awakes,
In water's grip, the earth remakes.

Every droplet tells a tale,
Of whispered winds and ships set sail.
Together they compose a song,
In harmony, where all belong.

As puddles form, reflections grow,
Embracing both the high and low.
The symphony of life now weaves,
Through every heart that joy perceives.

Palette of the Tempest

Winds of fury, shades of grey,
Brush the skies in wild dismay.
Clouds collide, a vibrant clash,
Painting storms with every splash.

Lightning strokes in vivid white,
Coloring the canvas of night.
Each thunderclap, a sound divine,
Mixes colors that intertwine.

Darkness fades, revealing light,
In the chaos, colors bright.
Nature's palette, bold and true,
Crafts a masterpiece anew.

As the tempest starts to wane,
Rainbows arch, dispelling pain.
In the aftermath, peace will reign,
Whispers of hope in every grain.

Echo of the Rainbow's Heart

After the storm, a calm embrace,
Colors merge in a warm space.
Each hue sings of stories shared,
Reflections of the love we bared.

Gentle arcs across the sky,
Whisper secrets as they fly.
Each band connects the earth and air,
Echoing dreams that wander there.

From crimson blush to lavender,
Every shade, a sweet endeavor.
In the silence, hearts convene,
In the light, the world is seen.

As shadows fade, the dawn does part,
Radiating from nature's heart.
In every echo, hope shall sing,
Reminding us of joys in spring.

Luminous Trails on a Gloomy Canvas

Stars emerge in velvet night,
Guiding souls with gentle light.
Each twinkle tells of dreams yet spun,
In the dark, their stories run.

Moonlight drips on silent streams,
Painting shadows, weaving dreams.
Gloomy canvas, yet so bright,
With every trail, hope takes flight.

Constellations map the way,
To brighter lands where spirits play.
Though darkness wraps the world in fear,
Each luminous path draws us near.

In the silence, dreams awaken,
With each step, never shaken.
For every sorrow, light will chase,
Bringing warmth to the darkest place.

The Tremor of Colorful Rain

Drops of joy paint the street,
Vibrant hues dance, a warm greet.
Laughter mingles with the sound,
Joyful splashes all around.

Winds weave tales through the throng,
Nature sings a lively song.
With each splash, spirits rise,
Underneath the grayened skies.

Puddles form like mirrors, bright,
Reflecting wonders, pure delight.
As colors blend and twist anew,
Life awakens, fresh and true.

The tremor stirs and plays the heart,
In this canvas, we're a part.
One with rain, in hues, we find,
A world alive, beautifully entwined.

Breath of the Prismed Breeze

Whispers float on gentle air,
Carried softly, light and rare.
Kaleidoscopes in every sigh,
Colors blend and drift on high.

Through the leaves, the breezes play,
Nature's breath in soft ballet.
Each hue dances with the sun,
A radiant song, a world spun.

Faintest blush upon the morn,
Awakens dreams, a new day born.
In this glow, we find our space,
Cradled in the winds' embrace.

With every gust, the heart takes flight,
Into the warmth of fading light.
The prismed path, a journey free,
In the spirit's flight, we see.

A Chorus of Water and Light

Rippling streams in silver arcs,
Whispers of water, gentle sparks.
Together they sing sweet and clear,
Nature's chorus, pure and dear.

Light cascades on flowing waves,
Painting dreams that the river saves.
Every glimmer holds a tale,
In the harmony, we set sail.

Moonlight dances on the crest,
In this embrace, we find our rest.
Rippling laughter, glowing bright,
United here, we feel the light.

In the depths, reflections play,
The heart's secrets on display.
A chorus forms beneath the sky,
A symphony that will not die.

Dappled Melodies from Above

Sunlight filters through the leaves,
Casting shadows where it weaves.
In the dance of light and shade,
Nature sings, a serenade.

Birds croon soft, a lightened heart,
In every note, a work of art.
Colors sway, in harmony,
Dappled melodies set free.

Rustling breezes whisper low,
Telling tales we long to know.
Each moment holds a fleeting grace,
In this delicate embrace.

Above us, skies in hues so grand,
Every brush a painter's hand.
With stars as notes, the night descends,
In dappled dreams, the music blends.

Ethereal Streams of Light and Rain

Gentle whispers touch the ground,
As colors leap and twirl around.
Softened droplets sparkle bright,
Creating streams of pure delight.

From heavens high, the raindrops prance,
In rhythm, they perform a dance.
With every splash, a world reborn,
In light's embrace, new dreams are sworn.

Beneath the clouds, a canvas wide,
Where nature's secrets do reside.
Through every hue, a story flows,
In ethereal streams, the spirit grows.

As twilight weaves its golden threads,
In soft embrace, the daylight spreads.
With every breath, a melody,
In light and rain, we wander free.

Synthesis of Light in a Shower's Dance

Raindrops fall on thirsty soil,
With light's embrace, they twist and coil.
A symphony of sound and gleam,
Each droplet joins the joyful theme.

The sky, a painter, bold and bright,
Dances with shadows, day and night.
A fusion of warmth and cool disdain,
In this shower, let love remain.

Through vibrant flashes, colors blend,
A moment paused, the world's suspend.
Each shimmer tells of life's delight,
A synthesis of love and light.

In puddles deep, reflections gleam,
Where nature flows, we dare to dream.
With every rain, the heart takes chance,
In synthesis, we join the dance.

Cascade of Dreams in Vibrant Tides

On shores where whispers billow high,
The waves of dreams begin to fly.
In jeweled splashes, stories rise,
A cascade of hope beneath the skies.

With every pulse, the oceans roar,
Mapping the journey to distant shores.
Colors swirl in passion's tide,
In vibrant hues, our dreams abide.

The sun dips low, igniting fire,
As stars awake, we never tire.
In every crash, a chance to find,
The secrets of our heart and mind.

In twilight's grip, the world ignites,
With cascades of dreams, we've taken flight.
To chase the waves, a dance sublime,
In vibrant tides, we dance through time.

Hues Unraveled in the Soothing Downpour

In soothing rain, where colors run,
The palette blooms, a quilt undone.
Through tranquil drops, the world unfolds,
In whispered tales, the heart beholds.

With every hue, a story told,
As nature's brush begins to mold.
The sky weeps joy, and earth responds,
In soothing downpour, connection bonds.

A prism bright in lightly grey,
With every droplet, beauty sways.
In layers rich, emotions blend,
As hues unravel, hearts transcend.

Embrace the warmth of rain's sweet kiss,
In vibrant dances, find your bliss.
For in each storm, the world renews,
In soothing downpour, love imbues.

A Charmed Journey of Colors and Clouds

In skies where dreams begin to play,
The clouds weave stories, soft and gray.
Colors dance on the horizon wide,
A charming journey, where hopes abide.

Sunrise blushes, waking the day,
While gentle breezes guide the way.
Rays of gold through cotton bright,
A canvas painted, pure delight.

As daylight fades, the hues abide,
Twinkling stars in the darkened side.
Night's embrace holds colors true,
A charmed journey, forever new.

In every shade, a tale is spun,
Of colors melding, one by one.
Through skies adorned with twilight's glow,
A journey sweet, where dreams still flow.

Fusion of Elemental Beauty in the Mist

In misty realms, where silence breathes,
The elements dance beneath the leaves.
With whispers soft, the spirits rise,
A fusion bright 'neath silver skies.

Water weaves through stones so fair,
A gentle touch, a lover's care.
While winds carry scents from afar,
The beauty here, a shining star.

Earth holds secrets beneath the green,
In hidden places, yet unseen.
Flames flicker in shades of white,
A fusion of beauty, pure delight.

With every droplet, a story flows,
In nature's arms, the magic grows.
Elemental wonders, forever missed,
In the soft embrace of morning mist.

Shimmering Hues in Nature's Embrace.

In nature's arms, where colors weave,
Shimmering hues that hearts believe.
Each petal glows with sunlight's grace,
In every corner, a warm embrace.

Lush greens sway with the tender breeze,
Golden rays filter through the trees.
Mountains rise, kissed by the light,
Nature's canvas, a pure delight.

As rivers run with crystal clear,
Beneath the sky, we gather near.
The beauty here, a sacred space,
Shimmering hues, our spirits trace.

In twilight's blush, all comes alive,
A dance of colors, dreams revive.
In nature's grip, we find our place,
Shimmering hues in warm embrace.

Whispers of Color in the Storm

When storms arise, with thunder loud,
Whispers of color break the shroud.
Raindrops fall like liquid light,
Nature's art in wild delight.

Shadows play on the drenched ground,
The beauty here, profound, unbound.
Colors swirl in the tempest's breath,
A canvas painted, life and death.

Lightning strikes, a jagged spark,
Illuminating the soft, dark.
In chaos lies a vibrant song,
Whispers of color, fierce and strong.

As the storm fades, a rainbow arcs,
Painting hope with its vibrant marks.
In silence now, the world transforms,
Whispers of color in gentle storms.

Serenity's Palette in a Gentle Flood

A quiet stream flows by,
Whispers of colors bright,
Brush the canvas of the sky,
In soft hues of gentle light.

Petals dance on water's face,
Ripples sing a soothing tune,
Nature wraps us in her grace,
Underneath the watchful moon.

Raindrops paint the world anew,
In every stroke, peace resides,
Blues and greens, a tranquil view,
Where calm and beauty coincide.

Each droplet tells a tale,
Of fleeting moments, serene, clear,
In this palette, hearts unveil,
A dance of joy amidst the tears.

The Spectrum's Serenade in Soft Drizzle

As rain begins to hum,
A symphony of light unfolds,
In colors soft, we come,
Where every droplet holds.

Misty notes in pale embrace,
The sky tunes into a sigh,
Painting dreams that we can chase,
As watercolor clouds drift by.

Through the veil, a rainbow peeks,
Tenors of hope, high and free,
In gentle whispers, nature speaks,
A serenade for you and me.

Each splash a secret shared,
In a world of drifting hues,
Textures of love, fully paired,
A melody in morning dews.

Mosaic of Serenity in Falling Water

The brook weaves a tale so sweet,
Each drop a note in blissful flow,
Crafting patterns where we meet,
In tranquil moments, love does grow.

Cascades of memories, bright and clear,
Reflecting stories in sunlight's glow,
In the silence, whispers appear,
Each splash a reminder of peace we know.

Fragments of laughter in the air,
Fluttering leaves join the soft refrain,
Together, they nourish the gentle care,
In a mosaic where hope can remain.

Nature's palette, rich and vast,
In falling waters, life anew,
Each moment captured, destined to last,
A soothing dream in the morning dew.

Colorful Whimsy in Every Drop

In the dance of each small drop,
Lives a spark of playful cheer,
Painting rainbows that never stop,
In the laughter we hold dear.

Swirls of hues in wet embrace,
Every splash a wink from grace,
A joyful shimmer in nature's lace,
Where worries fade without a trace.

Puddles form a mirror bright,
Reflecting dreams of skies above,
In this wonder, hearts take flight,
A canvas filled with purest love.

Let every droplet fall and play,
In this whimsical world we share,
For in the rain, come what may,
Life's colorful joy is always there.

The Lightness of Being in a Liquid Canvas

In the stillness, colors dance,
Flowing softly, a fleeting chance.
Ripples echo, whispers of grace,
Every droplet, a gentle trace.

Beneath the surface, dreams entwine,
Every shimmer, a story divine.
Floating lightly on currents below,
Embracing the journey, letting go.

Brushstrokes fade into soft sighs,
Reflecting worlds where spirit flies.
In liquid depths, we seek the light,
A fleeting moment, pure delight.

Every wave, a timeless song,
In this realm, we all belong.
The lightness of being, a tender thread,
On canvas of water, dreams are bred.

Wandering Colors in the Storm's Embrace

Clouds gather, a painter's despair,
Brushes dipped in electric air.
Colors clash in a wild ballet,
Nature's canvas in disarray.

Lightning flashes, hues ignite,
Wandering colors in velvet night.
Storms whisper secrets, bold and fierce,
With every heartbeat, the canvas pierce.

Rains fall like notes in a symphony,
Tumbling rhythms set our spirits free.
Each drop a splash, vibrant and raw,
In storm's embrace, we find our awe.

Dancing shadows, a transient fame,
In chaos found, we're never the same.
Wandering colors, a spirited call,
In the storm's embrace, we rise and fall.

Harmony of Hues in Glistening Trails

A spectrum shines in morning light,
Glistening trails, a wondrous sight.
Colors weave in a tender embrace,
Binding all in an endless space.

Brush of nature, softly drawn,
A melody plays, a gentle dawn.
Each hue whispers stories untold,
In harmony's dance, magic unfolds.

From ochre earth to azure skies,
The world blooms bright, where beauty lies.
In every shadow, a moment shines,
Hues of life in perfect designs.

Glistening trails, where dreams compose,
In the garden of color, vibrant grows.
Harmony calls, a luminous trail,
In the heart of nature, we set sail.

Spectrum's Breath in Rainy Whispers

Raindrops gather on surface wide,
Spectrum's breath, a soothing guide.
Whispers dance on puddles deep,
Night's embrace, a secret keep.

Colors bleed and intertwine,
In rainy whispers, life aligns.
Each droplet holds a world anew,
In gentle storms, the heart finds truth.

Softly sighing, the earth weeps,
In every color, memory creeps.
The air is washed, the mind set free,
A symphony played, just you and me.

Spectrum glows in twilight's grace,
In rain's envelope, we find our place.
Breath of colors, dancing light,
In rainy whispers, hearts take flight.

The Poetry of Atmospheric Dance

Whispers of wind through the trees,
Gentle sway, a rhythmic tease.
Clouds pirouette across the blue,
Nature's stage, a wondrous view.

Sunlight glimmers on the lake,
Reflections shimmer, ripples break.
Dancing shadows, a fleeting sign,
Nature's art, divine design.

Raindrops tap on window panes,
In soft cadence, sweet refrains.
A symphony in every breath,
Life's ballet, a dance of depth.

As twilight falls, the stars emerge,
Each twinkling light, a cosmic surge.
In the silence, the world takes flight,
The poetry of the dance ignites.

Merging of Light and Moisture

In dawn's embrace, the mists arise,
Where light and water softly ties.
Dewdrops glisten on the grass,
Nature's kiss, as moments pass.

Rainbows arch where sunbeams play,
Colors bloom in a bright display.
The air, alive with a fresh scent,
In harmony, the skies are bent.

Puddles mirror the clouds above,
A tender blend of light and love.
Every droplet tells a tale,
In this dance where dreams prevail.

As storms rage and thunder roars,
The merging magic always soars.
For in each drop, a story flows,
In the light, the moisture knows.

Joy Borne from the Gloom

In shadows deep, a spark ignites,
Hope's soft glow, amidst the nights.
The heartbeats fast, yet spirits soar,
From gloomy depths, we seek for more.

Laughter bubbles, breaking chains,
In darkest hours, love remains.
From sorrow's soil, blooms arise,
Beauty shines from tear-streaked skies.

Every trial, a lesson carved,
In joy's embrace, we're never starved.
With open arms, we greet the day,
Turning gloom into a brighter way.

So let the shadows come and go,
For in the depths, we learn to grow.
Joy, like a phoenix, takes to flight,
In every heart, a spark of light.

The Unseen Road of the Sky

Above the clouds, where dreams take wing,
An unseen road, a silent spring.
Stars like lanterns guide the way,
To secrets held in night and day.

The moon whispers tales to the breeze,
As constellations dance with ease.
Winds carry wishes, lost in time,
On this path, we dare to climb.

Each star a beacon, shining bright,
Illuminates the darkest night.
Communication with the divine,
In the vastness, our souls entwine.

Through every journey, vast and wide,
The unseen road, a cosmic ride.
In the skies, we'll find our place,
In the universe's warm embrace.

Traces of Color in the Rain

Raindrops fall with gentle grace,
Painting streets in hues embraced.
Each splash a whisper, soft and light,
A dance of colors, pure delight.

Under clouds, a canvas spreads,
Where dreams and memories are fed.
Bright umbrellas bloom on the street,
In this vibrant, rhythmic beat.

Puddles mirror skies above,
Reflecting moments, peace, and love.
In each glimmer, secrets play,
Evoking thoughts that drift away.

The world alive in muted tones,
Where nature's art forever roams.
Traces linger, soft and clear,
In every drop, a world sincere.

Harmonics of the Sky's Moisture

Hear the patter, soft and low,
A melody only rain can show.
Each note is a promise, sweet and true,
In symphonies born from skies so blue.

Clouds gather, a choir in flight,
Singing songs through day and night.
The air is thick with stories bold,
Of sunlit days and nights of gold.

Each raindrop plays its singular part,
Creating rhythms that fill the heart.
Together they weave a luscious song,
As nature's pulse beats strong and long.

In the hush, a world reborn,
As colors dance with drops of corn.
The harmonics of the moist embrace,
Whisper of life, a tender place.

Colorwashed Journeys

Through puddles deep, the colors glide,
A journey taken, side by side.
Each step an echo, a place well-trod,
In vibrant hues, the earth's facade.

Brushstrokes of sunset bleed anew,
Across the canvas, every view.
Golden pathways in the rain,
Leading hearts to joy and pain.

With every splash, a story spins,
Of stitched together losses, wins.
Colorwashed memories unfurl,
In every drop, a shining pearl.

As the world turns, the shades collide,
Creating tales where dreams abide.
Journeys in rain, a sacred art,
Colors merging, a tender heart.

Legacy of the Liquid Arc

In twilight moments, shadows cast,
A liquid arc, a spell is passed.
Rainbows stretch through stormy skies,
A legacy of beauty, it supplies.

Each drop a thread in nature's loom,
Weaving fate in vibrant bloom.
Gentle whispers, stories trace,
Legacy left all over the place.

Listen closely, hear the call,
From nature's heart, uniting all.
Through every storm, through every strife,
The liquid arc enriches life.

Hearts embrace the fleeting light,
As colors fade into the night.
Forever cherished, always near,
The legacy of rain we hold dear.

Vibrant Currents on a Glistening Path

Along the river, whispers flow,
Colors dance in sunlight's glow.
Leaves flutter down, caught in the breeze,
Nature's palette sets minds at ease.

Step by step on pebbles bright,
Reflecting dreams in morning light.
Waves of laughter blend sweetly here,
With each echo, banish fear.

Drifting petals, soft and light,
Tales of wonder, pure delight.
Every turn, a new surprise,
Magic captured in the skies.

In this moment, hearts collide,
As vibrant currents gently guide.
Together in a world so vast,
Creating memories that last.

Twilight Colors in a Festive Shower

As twilight dips, the colors blend,
A festive dance that will not end.
Shadows whisper tales of old,
While stars appear, bright and bold.

Raindrops shimmer, soft and clear,
Each one carrying hopes so dear.
Laughter mingles with the breeze,
In this moment, hearts feel at ease.

Candles flicker, casting light,
Creating warmth in the cool night.
Songs of joy fill the air,
A symphony for those who dare.

Underneath the evening's hue,
We find strength in dreams anew.
Hand in hand, we face the dark,
Together, we ignite a spark.

Echoes of Laughter in Misty Shades

In the mist, laughter rings clear,
Soft echoes weaving memories near.
Faces light up, glowing smiles,
Together we dance through winding miles.

Clouds wrap us in soft embrace,
Gentle whispers, a sacred space.
Footsteps marked on dewy grass,
Moments linger, refusing to pass.

Each heartbeat resonates strong,
An endless melody, a joyful song.
Through the fog, we find our way,
Guided by love that will not sway.

With every hug, every cheer,
The world unfolds, bright and clear.
In this symphony, we stand tall,
Echoes of laughter, binding all.

A Torrent of Echoed Rainbows

A torrent bursts, colors cascade,
Rainbows arch where dreams are laid.
Each drop, a story, bright and bold,
Promises whispered, secrets told.

Sky ablaze in vivid hues,
Nature's art, none can refuse.
Chasing rainbows, hearts set free,
Living in a tapestry.

Through stormy nights, we find our way,
Guided by hope that won't decay.
In every storm, beauty blooms,
Within the chaos, life resumes.

So let the colors dance and sway,
In the light, we find our way.
Together here, we paint the skies,
A torrent of dreams that never dies.

Adrift in a Gallery of Storms

Clouds gather, heavy the air,
Whispers of thunder, a wild flare.
Waves crash, dance in chaotic time,
Nature's heartbeat, a thunderous chime.

In the tempest, shadows play,
Figures emerge, then drift away.
Colors swirl in a fearsome flight,
Art of chaos, painted in night.

Lightning streaks across the sky,
Electric brush strokes, a violent sigh.
Memory lingers on each gust,
In storms we trust, in storms we must.

Adrift in tales of thunder's roar,
Each heartbeat echoes, wanting more.
Anchored in this vibrant strife,
Art unfolds, embodying life.

Flickers from the Sky's Tear

Stars wink softly, secrets to share,
Glimmers of light, floating in air.
From the heavens, a tear falls bright,
Illuminating the canvas of night.

Cascades shimmer, reflections dance,
In this moment, we take a chance.
To dream in colors, vivid and rare,
Flickers of hope, hanging in the air.

A gentle breeze carries their song,
Murmurs of magic, where we belong.
Every glint, a story to weave,
In the sky's tear, we dare to believe.

Flickers guide us beyond despair,
In their warmth, we find our share.
Underneath this celestial embrace,
We discover our true place.

A Choreography of Water and Light

Rippling reflections on quiet streams,
Nature dances in radiant dreams.
Sunlight glimmers on the surface fair,
A ballet of hope in the cool, crisp air.

Droplets twirl with a graceful sweep,
Echoes of laughter in shadows deep.
Water paints stories with every flow,
In intertwining paths, we learn to grow.

A symphony played by the wind and tide,
Waves move gently, with time as their guide.
In the crystalline shimmer, secrets find flight,
Where water and light become pure delight.

A choreography born of gentle grace,
Mirroring life in this sacred space.
We dance along, hearts open wide,
With water and light, forever tied.

Sunlit Tears on Canvas

Brushstrokes of gold across the day,
Sunlit tears in a vibrant display.
Colors harmonize beneath the glow,
Each drop a memory, soft and slow.

With every layer, a story unfolds,
An artist's heart in the hues it holds.
Canvas soaked in emotion's embrace,
A tapestry woven, a sacred space.

Bright mornings spill into dusk's embrace,
Moments captured, time can't erase.
A dance of light as shadows retreat,
In sunlit tears, life's pulse feels sweet.

With each glance, my heart starts to race,
Sunlit tears in this timeless place.
Forever painted, never to fade,
In the colors of love, I find my shade.

Harmony in the Glistening

In the dew of dawn, whispers sing,
Nature's voice, a gentle ring.
Leaves shimmer, life starts anew,
A dance of light in vibrant hue.

Birds take flight, on softest breeze,
Rustling branches, swaying trees.
Together they weave, a tranquil thread,
In harmony's heart, where beauty's fed.

Rivers flow with a soothing sound,
In joy and peace, the world is found.
Reflections play on water's face,
In glistening moments, time finds grace.

Beneath the sun, the earth does gleam,
Life embraced in a waking dream.
A symphony of heartbeats near,
In harmony's glow, all is clear.

The Laughter of Wet Petals

After rain, the flowers beam,
Petals glisten, as if in a dream.
Color splashes on the ground,
Nature's joy, all around.

Each drop dances, like a child,
Whispering secrets, sweet and wild.
A fragrance fills the heavy air,
Soft laughter drifts without a care.

In the garden, soft and bright,
Wet petals sparkle in the light.
They sway gently, side by side,
In their beauty, we confide.

As sunlight warms the glistening crowns,
The world awakens, laughter resounds.
In every bloom, a story tells,
Of joy and life, where wonder dwells.

Rain's Chromatic Serenade

Rain begins with a gentle sigh,
Draping hues across the sky.
Each drop falls, a different note,
A melody that seems to float.

Silver strings of water weave,
Colorful tales that make us believe.
Pattering softly on rooftops play,
As nature unleashes her vibrant display.

A canvas painted, rich and deep,
In each drop, secrets keep.
Through puddles, reflections shatter,
A rainstorm sings, nothing else matters.

In the storm, we find our peace,
Where worries fade and joy won't cease.
Every splash, a joyful cheer,
Rain's serenade, for all to hear.

Light's Journey Through the Gust

A beam of light through branches waves,
Dancing along the wind's cool braves.
In golden rays, the shadows play,
Whispers of dusk invade the day.

Each gust carries stories anew,
Of distant lands and skies so blue.
With every breeze, the colors blend,
A journey of light, we all commend.

Through rustling leaves, the sunlight streams,
Painting the ground with flickering dreams.
As twilight comes, a promise glows,
In this dance where nature flows.

Together they weave, a tapestry bright,
Of light and wind, in pure delight.
With every gust, the world's alive,
In the journey of light, we thrive.

Light's Caper in the Cloud Dance

In the sky, the colors swirl,
Bright hues in a twirling whirl.
Sunbeams flicker, shadows play,
As clouds dance in a bright display.

Whispers of the breeze take flight,
Chasing dreams through morning light.
Nature's stage, where spirits soar,
A caper that we all adore.

Every moment, a magical tease,
Guided gently by the breeze.
Softened edges, silhouettes form,
An ever-changing, vibrant norm.

Joyful hearts as daylight fades,
In twilight's glow, the magic wades.
A canvas wide, painted bold,
In light's embrace, treasures unfold.

The Weeping Palette of Nature

Colors bleed from nature's art,
A weeping canvas, a tender heart.
Rich greens meet the skies above,
In every hue, a story of love.

Raindrops kiss the petals soft,
Each droplet bids the blooms aloft.
Painting landscapes, full of grace,
Emotions captured in time and space.

Beneath the pines, the shadows lie,
With whispers of the passing sky.
Nature weeps, but spirits lift,
In her beauty, a precious gift.

The palette shifts, from dark to light,
As day gives way to gentle night.
Through every change, a cycle blooms,
In weeping hues, the heart resumes.

Fluidity Beneath the Glistening

Rippling waters, smooth and free,
Whispers dance in harmony.
Beneath the surface, secrets flow,
In the glistening, mysteries grow.

Gentle currents shape the land,
A steady force, both soft and grand.
Mirrored skies, where dreams collide,
In fluid grace, the world will bide.

Sunlight sparkles, shadows weave,
Nature's fabric hard to believe.
Every drop tells tales untold,
In this river, both warm and cold.

Through valleys deep and mountains high,
Life's essence flows, never shy.
With every wave, a journey starts,
In the glistening, fluid hearts.

Rhapsody of Falling Light

Sunset hues begin to spread,
A rhapsody where dreams are fed.
Golden rays, a soft embrace,
Painting dusk across the space.

Each flicker sings a lullaby,
As daylight whispers its goodbye.
Shadows stretch, blend with the night,
In harmony, they take their flight.

Stars emerge, like jewels bright,
Glistening treasures in twilight's sight.
A symphony of worlds aglow,
In falling light, a soft hello.

Beneath the canopy, stillness reigns,
Feel the rhythm of nature's veins.
In this rhapsody, hearts take flight,
As dreams awaken in the night.